The Patriot

The Patriot

*Poems by
Christopher Davis*

The University of Georgia Press
Athens and London

Published by the University of Georgia Press
Athens, Georgia 30602
© 1998 by Christopher Davis
All rights reserved
Designed by Betty Palmer McDaniel
Set in ten on thirteen Weiss by G&S Typesetters, Inc.
Printed and bound by McNaughton & Gunn, Inc.
The paper in this book meets the guidelines for
permanence and durability of the Committee on
Production Guidelines for Book Longevity of the
Council on Library Resources.

Printed in the United States of America
02 01 00 99 98   P   5 4 3 2 1

Library of Congress Cataloging in Publication Data

Davis, Christopher, 1960–
   The patriot : poems / by Christopher Davis.
     p.   cm. — (Contemporary poetry series)
   ISBN 0-8203-1991-0 (pbk.: alk. paper)
   I. Title. II. Series: Contemporary poetry series
(University of Georgia Press)
PS3554.A9334P3   1998
811'.54—dc21   97-49513

British Library Cataloging in Publication Data available

To the memory of

Ben, my brother,

1963–1979

> . . . . the potency of the image is created partly by the possibility of its enduring. And, of course, images accumulate sensation around themselves the longer they endure.
>
> FRANCIS BACON

*omnia fanda nefanda malo permixta furore
iustificam nobis mentem auertere Deorum.*

CATULLUS, *Poem LXIV*

Acknowledgments

The poems in this collection have appeared in the following publications:

AGNI REVIEW: "Commencement Ode," "If You Love Something, Let It Go," "A Costume Straitjacket's Black Sleeve in Armoire Shadows"
AMERICAN POETRY REVIEW: "Sunday Afternoon, after a Funeral, One Can't Change?"
AMERICAN VOICE: "God's Cut-Off TV Screen's Vanishing Mirror Seems an Unshared Point," "A Babel Scraping His Blue Eye"
ANOTHER CHICAGO MAGAZINE: "Savior Fatso, Semi-Fascist"
ANTIOCH REVIEW: "Debt Is Survival's Ringing Phone"
BELLINGHAM REVIEW: "Arroyo Seco"
BLACK WARRIOR REVIEW: "Endlessly Rocking," "His Caul Put Down Outside His Tomb," "Tusks of a Forklift, at Head-Level, Prod through Shadows," "To the Queen of Tragedy," "Good Friday," "Voice against Christ from Inside a Clock Mask"
CALIBAN: "A Fallen Candle at the Center of Our Picnic"
COLORADO REVIEW: "How Can I Turn Off This Engine Now?", "A Soft Mad Voice through Black Lipstick," "Phaeton," "Loving This World without Tenderness," "The Red Dust Flesh as Brand New Filter"
CONTROLLED BURN: "Body and Land Are Not Different," "A Virgin Nymphomaniac as Antenna"
DENVER QUARTERLY: "To One Dead Boy," "Nevermore"
HAYDEN'S FERRY REVIEW: "Rapture"
INDIANA REVIEW: "Atlas and Mary, If Thy Son Lives, Where?", "Asking to Be Useful Somewhere Near the End"
INKY BLUE: "Duende," "Atlas Narcissus"
INTERIM: "To the Consumer," "A Mighty Pen Points Out a Private Eye?"
IOWA REVIEW: "Trying to Flee a Dark Bedroom," "Trying Not to Tease Him"
THE JOURNAL: "Silent Hymn," "A Soaking Flag," "Lovesong to an Empty Room"
MISSISSIPPI VALLEY REVIEW: "Dirge to Myself"

NORTH AMERICAN REVIEW: "Let Go the Ghost of Icarus"
PLOUGHSHARES: "Genesis," "The Patriot," "Aborted Fetus"
RIVER CITY: "Little Crisis Framed in My Window"
SONORA REVIEW: "To the Voice of Hart Crane's Mother"
VOLT: "The Recessed Self as El Dorado"
WILLOW SPRINGS: "In Effigy"

Some of these poems appeared in a limited edition chapbook entitled *Independence News* published by Sandstone Press in Charlotte, North Carolina. "Duende" and "Trying to Flee a Dark Bedroom" appeared in *Things Shaped in Passing: More "Poets for Life" Writing from the AIDS Pandemic*, published by Persea Books. "Commencement Ode," "If You Love Something, Let It Go," and "A Costume Straitjacket's Black Sleeve in Armoire Shadows" appeared in *On the Verge: Emerging Poets and Artists*, published by Faber and Faber/Agni Review Press. Special thanks to Timothy Liu, Deanna Campbell, and to the late Henry Sauerwein Jr., who directed the Helene Wurlitzer Foundation of New Mexico in Taos, where many of these poems were written.

Contents

Trying to Flee a Dark Bedroom   1

One
To the Consumer

Sunday Afternoon, after a Funeral, One Can't Change?   5
Debt Is Survival's Ringing Phone   6
Endlessly Rocking   8
Silent Hymn   10
A Soaking Flag   12
His Caul Put Down outside His Tomb   13
Tusks of a Forklift, at Head-Level, Prod through Shadows   15
To the Consumer   16
Loving This World without Tenderness   17
How Can I Turn Off This Engine Now?   21
Dirge to Myself   23
Trying Not to Tease Him   25

Two
To the Queen of Tragedy

Genesis   29
Little Crisis Framed in My Window   30
A Costume Straitjacket's Black Sleeve in Armoire Shadows   32
Voice against Christ from inside a Clock Mask   35
To the Queen of Tragedy   36

Aborted Fetus   37

Let Go the Ghost of Icarus   38

A Fallen Candle at the Center of Our Picnic   40

To One Dead Boy   41

Duende   42

Atlas Narcissus   44

The Recessed Self as El Dorado   46

Arroyo Seco   48

Lovesong to an Empty Room   50

Three
To the Voice of Hart Crane's Mother

The Patriot   55

Good Friday   56

Rapture   57

Commencement Ode   58

Atlas and Mary, If Thy Son Lives, Where?   60

Phaeton   62

Nevermore   64

If You Love Something, Let It Go   65

In Effigy   67
1. Hell
2. God against Christ
3. Heaven

Asking to Be Useful Somewhere near the End   69

A Babel Scraping His Blue Eye   70

God's Cut-Off TV Screen's Vanishing Mirror
Seems an Unshared Point   72

Body and Land Are Not Different 74
A Mighty Pen Points Out a Private Eye? 75
To the Voice of Hart Crane's Mother 77
Savior Fatso, Semi-Fascist 79
A Soft Mad Voice through Black Lipstick 81
A Virgin Nymphomaniac as Antenna 83
The Red Dust Flesh as Brand New Filter 84

The Patriot

Trying to Flee a Dark Bedroom

We could
have death, turning on
a see-through globe's lightbulb, our small reach
expanding over contoured
continents. Rubbed between fingertips, the Andes.
The spine's gone. Then the Rockies. Nevada's desert, glowing
red around this palm, feels
like sun-crumpled leather. Maybe it is
all overheating
from the core out. This afternoon, late, the heat needled
a private's dust-brown back
until he squirmed, naked, boring
down into
the rough, dry grass, nailing
a hunger burned by ants
into a grave's eye.
Failing to.

One

To the Consumer

Sunday Afternoon, after a Funeral, One Can't Change?

Mourning flies weep from a fig tree's shadowed heart.
Maybe he'll hide himself against the trunk for years.
A sweet scent swells, through the dense leaves, out
into breath—each rotting self joining a sum flies can't
resist, swimming down to sniff it through dark leaves.
He feels like any lonely boy, pushing down branches, reaching

in. Something hisses. The hand flies
back. A spider mounting a stung fly?
Through a cool stickiness called green, it smells his heat.
If, say, the savior father pruned its home, moving that hand,
    the revenge gloving frozen nerves, would
the widow's venom
choose? Trembling, as he trembles, in nude fear, whom would
    it see?

Still-life, on the white, gold-flecked Formica, of bright apples.
His brother's gone. This is a quiet meal for three.
Those rotting figs smelled of warm perfume, aftershave—
if he wept, no one would sniff death, not as he has. They'd
    seem cold.

Shouldn't food steam, fading, let him cry? He tries to mumble
I can't think straight, let me be.
Grieving mothers never whisper, *pass the salt.*
He needs to die. Her eyes are closed. He can't grow up.

Debt Is Survival's Ringing Phone

Tonight, you're frightened. Talking
with anyone, even yourself, makes you feel
too much—anything—and reminds you
of a driver:
heart attacking him, he rammed up
onto a sidewalk—he couldn't help it—charged
a crafts fair and killed his brother.
Was he evil? Is he you?
His lost foot dancing on the high beam's silver nipple, not
the brake, a flood of sunbeams nuking
(through the dusty windshield)
breath into his throat, burning
his clenched eyelids, could
he care?
Their screaming a red blur beyond the glass.
Against the wheel, his ribs pierced in.
The dark pennies spilled from his slack mouth.
Life's lightning, breaking
in a boy's spine shattering
against a headlight, enters
you, your eyes and mouth—
On your quaking knee tonight, a palm. Your present
friend's. You and he are huddled side by side, stoned
to the world, to the yellow
overhead warmth raining down; you're staring
into, not beyond, the black window.
Mute frost whitens the numb glass.
Against your ribs, his chest breathes on.
Outside, a shivering
new savior, penniless—

curled up in a dumpster in your head, unborn, snipped
from man's voice—is your keeper, wrapped
in headlines he can't feel, a green dump truck coming
without warning.
That's your fault.

Endlessly Rocking

1.

Five A.M. He'd had red hair. The taxi tiptoeing up Park
 Avenue alone.
As dawn bleached night, light's cavity
seemed everywhere, entrenched, each stoplight yellow to the
 end.

The minutes die. Naked, alone, tired
from random chitchat, his thought lives on. I rise.
Leaning sadly in the doorway to the bathroom, eyes trained
 in, seeing

his spine bared to me a few breaths before he died, spraying
Lysol into the space heater's glowing coils. (A fireball
had spit, and for the moment had obscured him.)

2.

Sleep? Massaging closed eyes, *breathing*
sinking into the last breath, hadn't the closeups
of the true knife seemed as real?

Out through the lit red Golden Gate Bridge, its trembling
 struts, a ghost gulls East
into the roar where night's still water.
A Bowery babbler lights morning trash for warmth.

Staring down from my steamed window into traffic,
every light from end to end a pasture green,
a sky of snowflakes melts away, touching those heads.

3.

sniff brother the rising smoke of leaves and hurt
the ghostly body against plateglass mind rubs
quietly rhythm mourning its linked sounds

kiss the red rose hearing yourself
whispering help with that last breath
fanning this burning tongue whispering hello

Gathering high at mirrored tops of the skyscrapers blued by
    dusk clouds touch their forms
in a high desert mountains wait for us to die

4.

as snow fell quietly on blue peaks dry graves knew rain

Silent Hymn

Pure sky, blue and cloudless, without end.

Late afternoon slants
across a range veined with old snow
                (the dark blue peaks
almost the ebony of night's outer space)
        ringing a field's far edge, then
the faded green of the tall fennel
        beyond barbed wire a magpie folds to
nearer you,
        reader,
                its feathers
                        black and white and blue.

In a ditch, the snowmelt
whispers. On the far bank, across from you
crushing wild sage and sniffing deeply, a
splintered cross
marks that old grave, white paint almost gone, termites
having nibbled ragged the neck
and the two wrists, pink
teacup roses hanged
around it at the throat, name
of the father
eaten off:

        your mother
kneels behind it, facing you. Black wash of hair hiding
her face, yet her neck bent, she must be staring
at her lap, arms warm around him, fingers playing in-
to the bouquet, into

herself, hands
entwined there at last. She moans softly. Her throat trembles.
Inside her, grief is pleasure.
A three-legged dog, slumping
through the point where wire has fallen, enters
the field, one broken body dis-
appearing behind a swell:

in this pink twilight all there is
                              is the night coming, black
and strong. Once you leave here, water so cold
         bones seem to hurt
shall be stepped into,
                  not across.

A Soaking Flag

Syntax, stitching ears, seems a blurred verb. Making
an entry into grief seems suicide, a quiet surrender
in the skull's smoking field lost by the noun, sweet
satisfier, its dead leaves used, rubbed
up against their harvester
the sentenced myth, creation
building nothing, noun piled on
noun, assembled lines falling away

into blue shadows, the curtained study's puddles, a dusty
cake topping the silenced, dark TV. Dear lonesome diary,
isn't this junk dead, its round screen blinded, the shiny
murk reflecting a closed door behind my mask? Dying
can't seem peace, can't feel so real, the mirror mind
imploded everywhere, its red spattered around this living
room. Ear of dust, I
beg you. Stay.

His Caul Put Down outside His Tomb

> *I have returned to my senses and regained*
> *my normal state*
> BHAGAVAD GITA, XI

Isn't it rich? Aren't
we a pair? Father?

Through the bonewhite walls, the living room seems
full of passed-on shades, your hi-fi re-

peating dead crones, high and whiney, deeply
throaty, drowning in the seablue sculpted pile.

Handwashing against me at the clogged sink, my other's
skeleton enwraps me: we're a root-veined stump. Turning

this globe, parting me from my keeper's black sockets,
nature's icepick cottonmouth stare tears open heaven

between us in breathless air. Shoulders touching,
trembling, nude foreskulls rubbing, cracking

up, my dream angel's regard flashcube bright,
your wife smiling upon our beach blanket of love,

can't three viewpoints fuse, turn death's mask in?
Nothing in grief's glare says not to try,

after all, pop, thy music mute, his wombs
shaded, two round silver dollars mirroring

sound's dead sea, burning
its impetigo crusts of salt.

Tusks of a Forklift, at Head-Level,
Prod through Shadows

Flesh-blond sacks of chalk dust taste like wafers
in this raw materials warehouse dark with sleep
behind shut firedoors, behind eyelids.

Between full skids of bodies ten layers high,
at a skid's foot, a slumped sack, bursting
open:

gently rubbed between the thumb and index finger, chalk feels smooth
like a cold ash,
fingerprints being destroyed between the tips.

Can't, of course, sniff the far sea,
not through the mildew-scent of colloids.
Smell the cold bay?
A ringing phone in the front office.
Dry in cardboard, egg powder smells like cardboard, wet.

Does the perfume of what's twisted in this ashtray cling
to God?

White noise
turned low, broken into by a static-broken newscast.
Someone forgot a radio?
The tool room door shut, its padlock closed,
no light escaping through the crack
between the threshold and the door,
God seems trapped inside,

trying to give up.

To the Consumer

Dried mice retreat to nests
to crumble. Dust can't be sniffed.
It hides. Overhearing trash
sacks crash and beercans clatter,
please, inventor and investor, enter
naked. Tremble. Finger
up the light. I'm your bruised wife
laid curled in trash, a skyblue Valium
in her fist. Let poison tears
invade your throat. Sniff
dead turkey. Eat
dependents. Gag.

Loving This World without Tenderness

1.

It's not so cruel the guard took his Y membership away.
A potential intellectual, he wanted too much to seem sacred,
to be the whole basketball team's scared girlfriend.

They never saw him clap
a quaking palm over his gasp
as their ribs crashed.

They, too, flung the brown orb carelessly away,
their soles shrieking like crows against the court's wheat-gold wood,
his eyes orbiting back into his skull,

half-seeing a black beak peck
through fat-white mist
at that pane high over men's heads.

Arms hooked over the crossbeams
of the torso-twisting tummy tightener by Nautilus,
rubber pads shoved up into his pits,

he let his exiled third eye wander across the crowded, quiet gym.
Blue eyes surfaced between far out cheekbones, froze
quickly, the hot breath flooding

from that mask feeding him life.
A Baptist missionary begged that he be banned,
the Bhagavad Gita having fallen from his sweatpants.

That last morning, thrashing laps,
he bumped his soft spot on the lane's end.
Raising his wet head up out of chlorinated tears,

the overhead tube lights raining fluorescence on wave facets,
he saw heaven's white saber slicing
in through skyblue tiles.

He cradled his crying face
inside his palm's open prayer,
whispering, "Back off now, God, I want to live."

The redheaded
lifeguard, not knowing
what to say, tiptoed away.

2.

Vacationing on Key West
he peeked through tanned legs
of ice cream-eating passersby:

a bag lady, wrapped in a gray blanket, was hunched
dreaming against a beauty parlor's display pane.
The hairdresser came out with a green hose,

screwed it onto a faucet beside the door,
watered dust from the sidewalk, sprayed
a white lunchsack in the gutter out

onto black pavement and, suddenly
laughing, shot his stream in her face.
He washed out her screaming mouth.

He blasted her back. She tumbled
onto black pavement, the tattered
blanket a mourning dove's shattered

wings. She scampered to beach sand,
him chasing her, laughing, till
she crumpled out of hose range.

Noon's blaze dried her face without tenderness
intended. The cone-gnawing emperors
must have assumed there'd been just cause.

3.

Camping across Kansas, alone, pausing at a farm nuked
by a twister, he quietly flinched, fear hidden in fear.
A street sign, bent into a jawlike semicircle, bit

the torn topsoil, the name buried.
Snapped powerlines like silver nerves flung
down straight over the flattened-

forward grassblades sculpted the idea of the wind's force.
A tractor, smashed, dropped. A splinter pierced the tire cover,
penetrating thick black rubber treads beneath it.

In a shattered grove, a tiny scream touched him:
a bit of plastic caul, thin as a fly's wing, stretched
taut between two twigs, mourned in the breeze.

Rectangles of tin siding, ripped from sheds, wrenched
by wind, cried softly now, hanged like antelope
from cottonwood branches they had flayed of bark and maimed.

One strip, twisted around double, wrapped about a cracked, bent-
down bough, looked like two swept-back Nike's wings
or like a scarf tossed in the breeze flirtatiously

and snagged. Thank God funny farmers found him
trembling in a lonesome melodrama called God's force.
Shared visions leavened the dread. Four cows flew

and two survived. Pop stayed above ground, laughing,
they said, at a neighbor's grain silo exploding
orgasmically inside a half-mile-wide funnel.

Rooster guts got sucked out. Turkey hens got plucked.
A roll of white Charmin never broke, unravelled gently
through the upstairs john window, threaded gracefully

around three treetops. From under the blown barn's roof,
its planks chucked back to mud and birdsong, the 4-H project sow
and her two piglets tiptoed, unhurt, screaming, the aftermath

of tragedy two brothers laughing, sometimes, after all.

How Can I Turn Off This Engine Now?

This evening, fear and grief grabbed me again.
Watering round evergreens out here, in front
of our ranchhouse, I surprised those two boys,

that redheaded brat, my murdered brother,
and that shuffling, sneering thug,
that Chicano who knifed Ben,

giggling on my station wagon's front seat,
diddling with the dashboard clock, fiddling
with the radio I guess I had left booming.

I lobbed rocks toward the cracked windshield.
They laughed. I screamed, "Split!" They laughed.
I shuffled inside, praying they would go home.

Later, I needed to pick up my holy father
at the airport. I delayed, a sad Atlas
moping in an orbit around the kitchen,

eating bitter leftovers out of a coffee mug,
shoulders shrugging under the glowing ceiling,
a headache angel screaming, "Die, die!" in my skull.

I craved scraping that fluorescent light off of me.
It made my white skin feel too cold.
They're still out there, that murderer

and that bloody-haired teen angel, outside
this car, jeering at me tucked down cowering
inside it, arrested behind this wheel,

helpless to abandon the front door I left unlocked.
How can I switch off this engine now? I can't rise
from this womb, shiver out there, come back in alive,

leave. This is hell. I got no choice.
Crazy mad, I shepherd that redhead
around the cul-de-sac driveway.

His gentle profile turned screaming to me,
his opened mouth smiling as he's sucked down
into that black grave under my headlights,

his cage snapping loudly under my black tires,
he cries for the mercy he can't get from me,
I who never gave myself mercy after he died,

I, who, like you, feel as if being happy
is like fumbling with some other tongue.
The lucky figure it out, how to forgive

this cruel world.

Dirge to Myself

This Brooklyn fairy, Walt Whitman and I trekked
toward the Z Train in the rain, I
about to barely make it to the airport,
some waiter deep in the subway station
plucking from a banjo slow
sad "Silent Night."

We came across a multitude of lawn-and-leaf bags
burst open
before a closed-down Photomat,
the unclaimed exposures aborted
out onto black asphalt,
the curb's drain clogged,

all us sheep
pausing to kneel,
scrambling for these shields.

Here's one of Mick,
mike clutched
up against
his lips, his hips twisting
in front of upstaged chums.

Try this one, taken
in some Motel 666.

It's of a page, a boy
squatting cross-legged,
his turban a terrycloth towel,

his member drooped between bare knees,
a wood flute poked into his sweat-silver lips,
a snake rising to his chin,
his mask as pale as milky marble,
his eyelids closed.

We felt tomorrow's chill fire dawning.
My friend and I eyed one another hungrily,

each frightened to turn
his smile away.

Trying Not to Tease Him

Walt, were you the last guy
capable of loafing out his brains
this wilting dusk,
on this dyed-red land killing quiet minutes

tiredly noting your reflection in some shoe store's silent window,
OPEN 24 HOURS
JUST TO SERVE YOU like my nametag
on the shut door?
Several phantoms testing traction in our image

—When the last sneaker is picked, won't death divide us?
Every store raped,
not this mere chance cheek our ghost dry-humps.
When I can find no hungry mouth to gag with fear?

I'd like to feel that, one saved life.
I'd like to save it.
For a change.

Is that boy dead, so pale
in a red wig with girl's black ribbons,
staring at my man-boned deathmask in the glass,
his right shoulder nudging my spine?

Even my name seems a sad lie.
The closing clerk fingering the lightswitch,
the drag queen smiles and goes.

Perfected Mortal,
will your Great You think death tasty?

In a few seconds
God'll suck into his dark hole Earth's lone outline

and God's you.
You're weak America
I wish I didn't love, me
in red drag thrown on to flash in your groin *wait,*
a pale boy begging you *don't die, Walt,*
in my kiss,
gone like this:

Two

To the Queen of Tragedy

Genesis

You and he and all your friends being herded
among wheat-tawny sheep down a country lane
waves of ferns topping embankments of gold dirt
hooves and heels raising a wafer-scented dust glow to the air
hard breath like butter gilding mouths
joining voices bleating like a choir
it's midmorning
the boys

rising free
into true blond-tenor notes no just one note
there is no harmony between them
blending like shepherds in old paintings with the sheep-sounds
the head in front of him detaching from its shoulders lifts and dips
slowing through a cool tunnel of bamboo stalks and shadows
why no sheep
maybe they're scattered maybe dead
orchids brilliant in black dirt beside the trail
Why such colors your voice whispers
I guess they're trying to attract mates
his glance means over his shoulder

you shrug
sort of embarrassed
drop where you see to the petals

Little Crisis Framed in My Window

Three men
laughing
around a boat's prow in her driveway, each man armed,
each shotgun broken in an arm's crook, all the men
wearing identical camouflage raincoats, each
making goose calls with a call clenched
in his fingers. She's behind them

and they know it. Leaning
relaxed in her doorway, letting
cigarette smoke rise from her two fingers
like a pistol, is she humming
nursery rhymes they half-remember
but can't name? The three seem

nervous, embarrassed. Air is sweat.
In the shadowy living room behind her back, a hidden TV's blue
    light throbs out toward two armchairs,
one empty; propped
in its twin's lap is a framed photo—
of a baby? She puffs out white smoke slowly.
She mouths something to the youngest, who just turned.

He seems so young, his raincoat gone. He pushes
his way past her. Into
her.

      He'd unbuttoned his shirt. His friends
shrug, and he's gone down a dark hall.
Probably it's work he'll have to do, lift
down some books.
They both doubt this. But not aloud.

Back to their cool, small cleanlinesses—
Loaded.
The two alone now.
Shy.

A Costume Straitjacket's Black Sleeve in Armoire Shadows

1.

Hiding from this life of murder
in a one-room nest of tan adobe
granted to him one wild summer,
the spoiled creator, bowing

like a found pilgrim, leans
into a Frigidaire. This erect
coffin's trapped starlight
chills looking-glass eyes,

numbing nerves in fingertips
snatching an iced apple,
lifting one last Bud Light,
his prints flayed off.

2.

Before bedtime, his pen mislaid, he raised
his skin-thin mattress for the first time,
exposing a whirlpool of black spiders
to the lamplight, then his scream;

dreams failing to come, he felt them swirling,
vacuumed up again into his hindbrain,
his head pounding the flabby pillow,
his deathmask imploding in sneezing dust.

Some other laughed. Blinds torn open,
he hanged his twitching frown out
through the frame containing this
targeted face, and there

3.

he was, inside the spilling lamplight's
center ring, the overhearer, squatting
on a squashed nest of scythed fennel,
his black leather jacket a prayer rug

spread out beneath his beak-sharp stare—
that girl-haired heavy metal drummer,
that starved trash practically fat
from stuffing his corpse plenty when it's free,

that Hollywood hustler who fucked drag queens
for the cameras, who hitchhiked from Tustin,
where his Mustang burst, to Taos,
a thirsty kitten howling in his pocket.

4.

Till it croaked. Face draped by a blond mane,
his snarl held back inside a twisted mouth,
his blue eyes silvery with sex, an Apollonian
Satan taking prey down,

he's doomed, of course, to thumb
into a knifeblade.
He hissed, "Don't you love leaving me
out here?"

That morning, on dust-gold streets, their eyes had hit;
the drummer's fist had opened, then
his palm had slid down, fingers fanning
across his own zippered bulge.

5.

"People out here," he hissed, "see
you're pretty crazy." The man wept,
go home, pirouetting his whole
body into its dark hole.

He paws his guest bed.
Cassette tapes clack.
He slaps his choice into its silver weapon.
Its voice box. Forever

hungry, keeping his trap locked,
dancing in the night against himself,
he'd howl as if wanted,
dead or alive.

Voice against Christ
from inside a Clock Mask

cruising a rest area, high

Golden beginning   let me feed alone, not paranoid
on locust whisperings through leaves   a tide of green
as delicate as a saint's tongues   pleasure nearing

then decreasing   God's breeze-waves dusty, hot, His breath
like cobweb fingerprints puffed obese, popped, drowning
my cheeks in fading strums   Afraid to rub   This detached head

Not of the wood tables, a lean savior rose, half-naked,
from among gobbling families: nodding his shaved skull,
he wove me deep into time's 3-D camouflage: turning

in hell, a green, leaf-ruffled limb his green stare masking,
his zipper's bulge framed in a peephole of green tongues,
his hooking forefinger beckons, does inchworm situps.

That's all, folks? To be seems ice wept into red palms
cupped around leaf-sludge of the duck blind Christ screamed
hollow like a skull a trembling twig popped his eye red

no choir of flies rises from a bent fag stamped in mud
a broken finger never opens the dark screen of swooning lids
forever falling no red blossoms death forgive us open mouths

To the Queen of Tragedy

Death perches reflected at my typewriter. Hold me.
Above my claws, in glass-fleshed night, the starlit
sockets sunk twixt ivory cheekbones, my mask glares
back. Headlights knuckle past the chin, outside.

(I tape a mother's sobs. Don't pick the receiver up.)
Dark-eyed wild sister rolling me around the rug,
you tickled me—I shrieked, "I pray thee, cease!"
I spun picture disc twelve-inchers of Bicentennial

parades, blurred sunsets twirled around a spindle.
I finally loved a book I'd bought called *Fine Art Slut*.
Some nights I'd race drunk through latent February ice,
the cold Bud silver in my throat, the breath withheld,

my own cigar smoke curing me, choking me up behind
the rolled-up panes. Enclosed, I sang too loudly.
Now, my friend, do charred fields of tobacco pool
like lungs of ink firing your hearse down interstates?

Aborted Fetus

Now that I'm gone, my pale boy-body near
your ear, my skull-white forehead used

up, out beyond the lamplight, a Cain
trembling on tiptoe, desperate, mute

in shadows, yearning down to hear you
read aloud from your stuffed armchair,

I'd die to point to the art print
lifted from the motel wall on the move

west, hanged again over cold ash, above
the mantle's crucifix and musket—a

dusty redcoat landscape of a
sunset slicing clouds of woolen mutton-fat

open, the silver rains cornered, the gold
blade harrowing in over the wild field,

dubbing the bent spine in a shepherd's
burlap shroud, his wingless shoulders

quivering, his nape bent down, eye turned
from us, his slowing heart trans-

fixed on shock.
Lambs chew his feet.

Let Go the Ghost of Icarus

Ideal mother, please stay far away
from this dead saint's bloodless lips.
At his kitchen sink Sunday,
the morning after, both men
kept mute, sighing
down into his cold cups.
Can others see under
a clay deathmask's stiff lip
the globe trapped in a skull?
Imagine it a flooded dome,
a cesspool of fluid shadows,
the black murk halfway risen
to the vaulted ceiling buried
under a knit brow, the eyelids
closed, the eyeballs bent
forever in, in love
with unreflected deeps.
Out in the brine, a swimming
soul thrashes
a whirlpool forward,
back a wake. Through our dim breath, the white
wrists flicker. The fingers knifing
down create fresh holes
in the wet shroud, the corpse
a spermcell working closer, ever coming, never
born, trapped
too deeply in death's promise
for becoming, never lifted out,
rocked on dry land, nor held

in warm arms even now, a wave responding
in thy mouth, a worried
prayer kissed
from your lips.

A Fallen Candle at the Center of Our Picnic

Far friend, I loved kissing your dead space, feeling
lonely nightmares melt away upon the closed buds
of the tongue, a demonstration of a surface

paradise. Most suicide seems
young, some punk preserving, in time's ice,
a cut-out heart. Coming from the edge, back

into the public park's green words, I recollect
these snake-necked geese gathered like suitors, nipping
popcorn from my lap; I kicked them from me, stuffed

and used. I can't drone on forever at a loom,
the flesh around this pumping blood
death's waiting nun, a sentenced fire.

To One Dead Boy

Spent a crisp morning in the horn, insuring
that the vanilla-toned fabric of the shroud
for another remains intact.

No thanks to you, I know:
don't harp haiku to debt collectors.
Life insurance men catch delicacies.

I guess I did pick
your white meat with typing nails.
How many more nights, hero, could I have unknit

sinews? Downstairs on hot tiles
the guests need red meat, tongueing
me down trembling

to their tusks.

Duende

One swollen evening,
warm rain flooded the gutters.
Dogwood blossoms had come out
over a wash of green leaves.
The world seemed quietly willing.
After a late, stiff lunch,
I lay back
and let a sick man
tenderize me, licking
my shoulder blades, my navel, my ass-
hole, opening
my body's envelope,
consuming the glue,
sheathing my flesh opener
inside his cheeks.
Waiflike, I prayed,
"Do you think it's all right,
your saliva?" "I think so," he smiled.
"Don't do something you don't want to do."
I touched his bald spot.
From his cock tip,
ghostly honey
oozed slowly
to the white shroud.
My white teardrop
plopped on my navel,
a pear tree petal
pressed to a wet windshield.
Rain throbbed on the roof.
Minutes throbbed on.
He handed me a poem about a rotting dog.

He brought me back. I collapsed
onto this green, bacon-scented sofa,
happy for a moment, wrapped
inside this stinking orb.
I puffed some grass.
Minutes pulsed past.
I felt like a dead bass
flopped out onto the sidewalk,
scales baked to a steel-gray leather
in the sun, a pelt of ants swirling
around me, nipping me, driving
me nuts, tucking
me in, my body
less strong than the mind,
the world around us suddenly
so young.

Atlas Narcissus

Everybody loved him,
finding him pretty
easy to cut off.

Feelings seemed, to him, a kind of weather,
worth no more notice than the rain,
no more lasting than the clouds.

When he tried hard to grow
a bean stalk from his navel,
he felt the axe buried in his torso:

his hurt buddy's pickup pulled out quickly,
its high beams impressing on the flesh adobe wall
the black shadow of a phone pole, a crucifix.

Inside him, had he died, the brave poet
marching, with a ghetto blaster shouting
from his shoulder, through the art museum?

Kissing the security guard's night stick?
White clouds like covered wagons crisscross the blues
above new herds of bison gnawing emerald blades.

In good time, a warm man's arms,
smelling of cologne and sweat,
wrapped his skull forever.

They oink, laughing, into each other's ears,
loving each death breath, each body
a pinpoint of resistance,

an obtuse old boar
squealing for life, feeling
a root of green lightning

fuse his scrotum to his soul.

The Recessed Self as El Dorado

The dawn you whispered, "Forgive me, I'm ill,"
I thought, Well, fate is fate.
I guess I had picked up
that hint about your will.

I bought some bread. I got lost,
free, alone, in this ghost town.
I counted the cassette tapes on the front seat.
I asked myself which dirge had been rewound.

Standing on a foundation of cracked cement
I gazed across the desert valley.
For one heartbeat
my breath felt like the wind.

We never climbed our peak.
I never typed our poem.
When I offered my hand
a magpie screamed away.

You'd needed help lifting down adobe bricks
from your brother's truck; you had coaxed,
"You must feel our clay's weight and texture,
rough and crumbling, at your fingertips."

Down at the hot springs, nude boys sprawled,
sunning, across flaming-hot boulders.
My body tingled, sinking
into warm, muddy fluid

flowing out through cracks
between stones nibbled
by minnows the same green
as the Rio's chill currents

soothing my flaming corpse
rafting face up past a cliff
where a Penitente bowed, frowning,
his hat brim pinched in his fingers.

When rain came, the sage smelled sweeter,
baptized in the cool tears of the father,
creator of this recessed place, this skull,
its heavy face always being wrenched loose,

readjusted, screwed
back down. I needed
you. I need you.
But I passed.

Outside the Center
my eyes tried
gnawing a wrapper
till my tears broke

and a black girl
leaning against a black payphone
shouted, "Look out!
Idiot! Look out!"

Arroyo Seco

I agreed to split the party early,
its dope smoke and drums, and trek
with my infected lover
across the moon-bright mesa
covered with wild sage,
blue-green, glimmering,
its odor bittersweet.

The Rio Grande slunk at the bottom of the gorge,
that dark crack before the horizon: fear
swelled in my endings like a river
when he slipped his lips over my finger.

I peeked back at the host's adobe hut.
A pickup pulled out from the driveway.
Its high beams impressed a phone pole's shadow,
like a crucifix, against
the flesh-colored garage.
The truck swung back
onto the road, tugging
the cross down into a
corner, shrinking it,
stuffing it into an

outlet. Independence Day fireworks exfoliated,
green leaves falling toward the school,
a red corolla blazing up, up, and away.

A comet danced like a spermcell across the sky's black shroud.

An empty lunchsack scuttled over my foot.

The next morning, a black mutt bumps
my coffeetable, spilling java,
just some juice boiled from black beans,
all over this white page,
empty, void of love,
the imprint of my friend's outer
ear still on my shoulder.

Fornication is just friction,
wrote Marcus Aurelius,
then a discharge.

Lovesong to an Empty Room

Among low weeds, a dandelion lays its full-headed shadow
    near a crack
in the naked concrete of what seems
the platform a gone furnace must have graced.

Sniff the wild sage, the rotting peaches.
In this midmorning glow tinted salmon by the most
    delicate smog,
don't you believe, now, in the gentlest refusal?

∽

The word *destroy* in orange spray paint on what charred
    cement blocks stand,
even the hint of four walls seems, you keep thinking, to
    accuse you.
Against the cliff's edge, the rear wall's hardly an
    outline, so step over

but below it, in the pool, a woman's sunning on her raft,
    the book she holds over her face shielding her eyes.
Then all the suburbs. And where they stop, sea begins,
    star-sapphire blue.
Isn't imagining a front door the way free?

∽

A field of sunflowers, their tall shadows a lace shadow
    among weeds
where their seeds fall, and a bent peach tree, its unpruned
    leaves so deeply wild

you can't see in. In your mind, your own voice calls from
   its sweet darkness.

A chainlink fence sags like a syntax
against honeysuckle bushes, against treetrunks, its poles
   fallen, the bottom links so easily
lifted: feel your sweat cool: in dusky green
don't more leaves fall than ever rot?
The avocado on your tongue tastes rich as flesh.

From the arm of a black bench, a rooster watches, its seen
   eye white, stabbing the shadows.
Its beak won't move. Is it not real? Near your shoe, a
   chick's corpse lies twisted.
It's white and frail—had it been pecked?—you touch it,
   trembling at the wetness of cold down.
Crumbling leaves and rustling feathers: head bobbing quietly
   toward you, a white hen—in her beak, held by the
   stem, a small, pink rose. You press
your cheek down in the leaves. Near your ear, a soft
   crowing.

In your closed eyes, under a blue and cloudless burning, an
   emerald hill.
At the center of a wet dichondra lawn,

red roses blooming all around it,
a hacienda, stucco walls a glossy white.

The steamed perfume of petals, and of green.
Behind drawn curtains, in tobacco-scented gloom around a
   glow, an empty armchair

being shown horrors God made, the volume low.
This is your throne, if you should care.

Garden scissors in your hand, your host's not God—it's
    only you
pruning the stems back, sprinklers chirping.

He'll never show more than his back. He wears no clothes.
If he hears trembling in these bushes, he won't turn,

his thinking focused on his fingers,
blades stained green.

Three

To the Voice of Hart Crane's Mother

The Patriot

Confused, using no maps, oldies
on fire, the would-be sister, Glenda, I inhabit,
drives a transformed hearse inside America
all night. Craving breast milk cut with booze,
seduced, come dawn, by Last Chance Supper Hut,
she catches Death (dressed as a stranger
in a red and white checked shirt) paying
attention: I'd got her self large
in pink panties. Our brother's body, rubbing
up a lit flashlight under
his own chin, bones jutting fierce over his glowing
dents of cheeks, black sockets blind, the tips
of his red curls torched devilish
from down below, our ghostly brother, just
last summer, trembled
in her ribcage, the one gray body
of starved pigeons closing in
across Trafalgar Square. Our father faked
flirty accents with the Bobbies. Every night,
candlelight laughing on the white walls
of rented rooms, our father failed
at pounding his wife's shadow
to a new shape. Kicked out from the nest
of her green sheets, a wild
turkey's skull drops, sharp
and hollow, through my fumble, and rolls
down to the slit foot
of the shut door, the fluorescent
milk-white other slicing
in. The halls of heaven must be quiet, and pure cold.
No turning knob. No flowered Oz. No hope of God.

Good Friday

Oleen's Lounge

Starver, you slipped alone and anxious to death's bar.
They'd done it all in blacks, mirrors and stainlessness.
On the lit dancefloor queens twisted like drugged worms.
One peered far into your recess, asking whom you played.

Those facing a purple bloom of fading feel okay here,
propped in wheelchairs, bruised sobbing shadows loving
life. At the bar, the skeleton you perched against slurred
I'm on fire, downing a double White Russian and Wild Turkey.

The lithe bartender begged him for painkillers, got some. You
too. Your friend turned, unveiling his rotting other cheek,
grinned: anyone that's been around's got it. Is disability

feeling the noisy flesh abandoning you? In the john mirror,
electric shroud Walkmanned around thy skull, the dead help say
stick out that tongue again, talker. Touch a white spot:

Rapture

Our father never looks up at the waitress, and he flirts with anyone.
The white surf creams around the driftwood clump, outside, beyond
smudged glass. No moon sticks out. The green, laminated menus closed
before us, and our fingerprints like too many dimes blurred together atop
photoperfect veal, he orders for me. Tastes the bloody wine. Scowls.
It must be cheap, sour. He rubs his eyelids (closed.) Won't say.

I'm in a subway station, *all alone and lonely*, kneeling unprotected, any
drunk, my own eyes closed. The indrawn piss-scents chill each
 thought.
Thin exhaust, mixed with bitter cigarette smoke, twisting free, tastes
 of quenched flesh.
From below, a trumpet's sob echoes around the dirty white tiles
 everywhere.
It's all the skull, that's how life feels. The groove I utter in here
 whines.
I'll always pray: from everywhere, from grease-black walls, rats could

sing out, sniffing down the endless rails into the tunnel's coming
 light

toward only you.

Commencement Ode

Fellow loser, there's no future?
Even the Bee Gees suffered in a world of fools,
staying alive.

So wear green pants,
sing foolishly, and dance
upon the grave of Andy Gibb.

Sweet spoiled sixteen, I got
from our broke pop
a band of gold. Now that he's

pawned, the half-drowned glint
in its star sapphire's skyblue eye
blinds like a blade.

Touch me, neighbor, staring
down at shaking fingers shielding
these shut lids: I'm half-hiding, my forelobe

bowed, attention curling up through dark meat tunnels,
scooting home across the black sea in this skull,
lost in Death's deflated star from even you.

Hear my stereo? On this front porch, I rise
from my knees, shoulders stooped, these plucked wings
spanning open to engulf the world's deep love.

I kick the door open behind me, sing softly
along, mixing up the words to vinyl prayers.
A squad car's blue light strobes away.

Turning inward, back into our living room,
I feel the TV's heaven-lapis screen flinch
as I ram this throbbing soft spot into life.

Atlas and Mary, If Thy Son Lives, Where?

Paul, another fine-cheekboned failure, we leased Eden
on the uplifted coast of California one whole summer, never

touching: once, tucked in my green sheets, eyelids
half-sealed, the gold sunrise igniting inward, realistic
like the backlit lite beer of commercials, clarifying
the white texture of the stucco prefab walls
and our paintings—only once—I hawked you
squirming yourself off like a serpent
on the leaf-beige couch, your bulge
in jeans rubbing away the rough surface.

I'd fingerpaint mother's wine-corrupted cheeks, sad
cul-de-sacs, a condemned bank tower blasted in
upon a flock. You hated waking me, my thumb
shocking my tongue, the day you split forever; you
with your minister father and your saint's name
did Elvis Rising Back from Hell as Christ Himself,
the fierce stare thine alone, ringed in black, a red
stormcloud clotting like lipstick aside green eyes.

We freed God in his cell, his forehead locked
against his glass pane's greasy blaze: *enter me*,
he'd lipped, a leather skeleton lonely in a piss stew.
Paul, recall him bowed in mourning? Raving marriage to the shower-
    bright emerald pasture as the sun fails? Mumbling
scat to five cows closing home, grave knuckles rolled into a fist,
    deep down, unseen, the lit ocean

a burning watch? An orphaned calf cried until dawn, found dead
with battery acid on its tongue. Moaning udders hadn't slowed,
pushed to be sucked free by machines, hand-perfected ghosts.

Naked, blind on warm beer, homeless toes iced in skull malls,
let us suck life, this red fee coughed into Your palms.

Phaeton

1.

I carry home an unclaimed wedding cake.
This was my dead friend's dinner of choice.
I eat much more than half of it.

Enough. Enough. I bear the rest outside.
I scatter his crumbs near the green hedge.
A gang flies down and gobbles the remains.

Crying slightly to blur things,
narrowing my black lids into slits,
hungry to suck heaven's white glow in,

I can't stab
with my orbs
the world's skin.

2.

I almost stumble—almost
break my own beak—
on a deposed mourning dove,
its gray wings splayed out across slivers of green glass in
    fescue blades,
its beak wrenched down, to the left, away
from white cloud-wisps, cataracts
of heaven in the blue blaze
its flat eye aims into

or through. It still wings
through the imaginary cumulus
between my cortex, my mind's mirror,
and my skull. In my living room
I stand here flapping plucked limbs up and down—

a little kid inside me,
abandoned on the beach, scrapes

his arms in the hot grains, making
an anti–snow angel, his skull bent

back, his hindbrain impressed
into a golden sand castle,

the sun, through his black lids, burning his tongue,
laughing blazing up out of his throat, his lungs.

Nevermore

To Lee Ki Young in Seoul

When I first showed up here, I said, aloud,
"My life seems visionary, half-real;
coincidences all *mean* something." How
dumb. The poet in pain with a nice smile,

the handsome homo with a withered leg,
without much chance left to love his large life,
had just asked me to read to him "The Raven."
His black bangs hang, bladelike, across his eyes;

he sits in lotus postures, legs an "X";
his fingers, curling in, touch his lifeline.
"I guess you have trouble expressing sex,"
he coughed; "you seem so weak, a helpless child—

why won't you touch this leg, this bone, on top?
I'm ill because you dream of touch, but stop."

If You Love Something, Let It Go

Homebound in a fuselage, tucked in, curled against you,
I watched God's words swim through black paragraphs
of the front page, ripples moving under a cloud's shadow.
A fortune fired up through my mind without my aid:

"Keep coming closer, kid, all should be well."
Once I'd come down, my babbling tongues
cut into by the secretary's flinch,
it hardly mattered if I lived or died.

I bore my tan cat to the gas chambers, I
who'd raised her to keep me up, flinging her
again, again, onto the wheat-gold floor.
She screamed all night to feel her four pads work again.

Hunched in her wire cage, screaming
down that hall, she screams in my dreams,
a secret friend I sing love lyrics to
who won't judge me from beyond me,

can't interrupt, want sex, or leave
language, a curled child buried
under the warm floor of a clay hut,
sheltered in the family's endless love.

Preen into this muddy fishpond I've inherited.
My mind. They say koi thrash around
down there, their gold wedding band mouths
gulping through the brown skin

when your forefinger taps knowingly.
In my neighbor's yard, he's ripped up
ivy tresses, revealing benign cactus tentacles
crisscrossing his dirt plot. Their one root,

we still can't find. Is breath a nest
between my hot heart and that raven paused
against me? Its skull keeps cruising
around this way, that way, famished

in the flyless air, its pecker
sharper than the beak between
my too-probing eyes, its black bod
lighter than these bloated bones,

its feathers sweating, gorged on evening heat,
glinting in the sunset as if faceted,
a coal ghost still inside a diamond,
its brand-new neon body electric being broadcast

on the black screen of these closed lids.
Burst me open, love, to life's dark dove,
that shadow clumped around
a wing-wrapped shadow,

stumbling up to this thumb and forefinger pincher
outstretched, offering these inky fingerprints,
that deadly little loved one flitting off
in awkwardness, in blessedness.

In Effigy

1. Hell

Club Body Center

Curled-up digits fisted mother's
other palm, opened, tender: did I peel
this soggy pelt from its stiff peg, ex-
posing the skull-white tiles? I skirt
my sex. In stinking showers, old Fat Tits
stares me down through crossing eyes, puckers
kisses through a black beard, kneads up suds
into a stinging cloud. A blimp pisses
lightning in silver rain. I shed
for him this swaddling shroud
from burning loins; my twisting
torso's fuselage, flicking
a pink tongue inside your ear,
savior, can't feel you near.

2. God against Christ

Tonight our pumpkin shares his flesh, reflected
carved out, thin and bitter in this mirror;
the bags under his stone eyes hint at black
bone under a memento mori mask.
He'd gag off its throat. He's blandly fingering
a talon down fat smog. Breathing is greed.
He's failed to starve our scorched earth free. Dead ends

rhyme. Remember form? Snuff-rhymes backward bend
to replace it with old books. So feel, free!

Your glassy fingers on cold lids repressing
upside-down faces deep in Isaac's face,
you'll dig his globes too, praying hold me back,
blind pits in this glaring black-white mirror
alive eight last gasps, sight rhyme rejected

3. Heaven

Feel how gouging future ghosts must hurt?
Burying this counterfeit beat can't help
punish its black bones brain-dead on this sheet,
each long flat broken line my signed-off self

slapped back to life. What higher paw designed
certificates of value, justified
if gold's elsewhere? This intricate resign,
the camouflage worn writing suggested.

The afterlife's this white skin in thy palm.
Each wrinkle smells sweet, dyed in evergreen,
in sweaty wallet-perfumed sage embalmed.

Go torch a dollar bill. Let ghost dates free,
its pyramid eye turned in, bricks strewn below,
black slaves wallowing in green undergrowth.

Asking to Be Useful Somewhere near the End

Do I, hearer, touch you? (Shut your eyes.)
I'm trying to stop singing

about insides, all
the self-sucking archetypes, puppet forms. Forget English.
Off apple pie the gold of dust, it tastes like Cool Whip.
I still, before a vast light slays cold
night, own a few moments
to grade poems
by those breeders of myself as President,
my sexy students—
those Confedcrate girls, those Vietnamese boys—
I feel I'm scratching with his pen Sam's drained corpse back,
or trying to,
lacking control.
Whom do I ape?

America died
never having evolved
(blown down curling to the dust, truly
      fucked, and weeping
         maybe dying
            under cool sky)
past a false self.

A white vein fading above geese; love, snow shall fall.

Our ideal union seems a new world,
long ago. Some good.

A Babel Scraping His Blue Eye

Curled up in his Mustang's rush-hour womb,
our male model presses back his tailbone
into the blood-red tuck-and-roll, a hard

belly. From the dash radio, an organ fugue
rubs all around his belly, rubs his button,
wooing down his foot on the gas pedal, a slow drone.

His focus jumps the road's trashy shoulder, to that mirror-
sided monolithic erection, that skyscraper, our flaring
windshield more sun passing all over its inferno surface.

If, like a tan snake, he climbed against sunset,
could he feel the day's heat shedding on his hide?
He'd rub each windowpane with a chamois,

impose his hologram through silver skin,
let it sink down through cold sweet semi-smogfree air
onto chilled leather with commercial planners,

their greedy forecasts lucid on their laps,
his flayed ghost immaterial, thus mute.
Through this windshield, his hot corpse can't

tap a warning. In the rearview, his whites
seem crystal paperweights, their orange pupils
daylilies exploding toward God's flashlight

from a fire core. Closing down his lids,
the blue tiles of a sex-dark men's room
glistening around him like pool water,

underwater floodlights won't burst sockets open.
Nostrils chlorine-seared, the skull pounding,
the last breath held, one swims and swims.

God's Cut-Off TV Screen's Vanishing Mirror Seems an Unshared Point

1.

Unlike talk, like prayer, this mist unravels
skeins of sweat across the lake's green skin,
censoring, then exposing, lanky scrub pines
quivering against white blossoms of dogwood
inverted deep inside Earth's paperthin mirror.

Is this some form of prank, or prayer,
this squirrel skeleton hanged overhead,
crucified upon a black telephone cable,
the twiglike arms hooked over that vine
our masks chitchat through silently?

Skull a blown-out walnut, socket-
holes bored for this giant rosary,
a conversation piece of deaths, see,
savior, my blackened delicacy grilled
under your stare, your high-noon fire.

2.

One spring night, I trembled frozen, caught
against white rapids in the eyes of a bone face,
an East Indian cab driver witnessing
at me more than an hour, ignoring
his idling livelihood behind him.

Smile against my face, he whispered,
Listen. When they reel Him down,

His visage all twisted in agony,
His fluorescent orbs exploding, moving
across each bearer's mask, down

to one's own quivering
lips, it's love, not death,
feeds us His burning
prayer to flesh,
this mortal form.

Body and Land Are Not Different

He kneels in a rice paddy, listening
to three old ladies chatting, squatting
in a circle, patiently, like poets, gathering

wild grasses into bundles, not as helpless
as a boy praying for a farm hand
to touch his soft hair.

Throughout the valley,
a train whistle sobs,
echoing inward off the cliffs.

Sunset glows on burial mounds
nobody has ever plundered,
torches of forsythia

descending into snowy
cherry blossoms hissing
in his loving memory.

At the outdoor market, a hog's vitals
dangle from a hook in the arrangement
they had had inside the torso:

the liver, smooth and brown,
below a heart covered with flies,
the end of the throat's hose gaping

open like a mouth, the whole body implied
by its essentials, its swiped image
wiped back onto the warm air.

A Mighty Pen Points Out a Private Eye?

Here he slumps, broken-hearted.
He tried to die. He's only started

losing Hangman,
playing against himself.

In this steak house, he holds out against love.
He mints elbow grease quarters on polyester wood.

He detected hate inside himself, wobbling
fucked-up among his flinching party friends,

the laughing room around him not all
there, but his, all his. Fucking,

crushed under a flesh billboard,
he muttered a vow of purity.

Isn't paranoia always lonely?
Doesn't strength come only

in public, in an adult bookstore, say,
the straight face maintained?

Should the word "manly" act
as some sort of grounding wire

hooking his brain to the balls
of that black stallion pausing

erect in the sunstruck meadow
on the green side of the tracks,

bowing to a root
it sniffs, it licks,

its hard-on hanging
between unbent knees?

Some soft thing touched down
upon his soft spot, once.

Isn't lust, like poetry,
a butterfly

riding an ugly
elephant, this industry

trampling our sweet body
it can't quite feel, can't feel for?

To the Voice of Hart Crane's Mother

Weeping lady, confidante and rival
shrieking fuck me, fuck you,
let's hop on our bikes.

Our handlebars curl in like
ram's horns. Over them, the shadows
of our torsos sway like snakes.

From the petting zoo,
twin howls arise, both
voicing a heat insatiable:

one from the huge-hipped hybrid,
half-Shelty, half—timber wolf,
lashed to a trash bin,

the other from a puma bitch
stretched out flat as road kill,
rubbing her hips against a bench.

That Penitente chapel looks forsaken.
Even its gang-related graffiti
shall fall, the outer plaster,

pink as flesh, falling away,
adobe bricks exposed,
eroded into each other.

Mother, lost in silence,
frotting against blood-soaked
inner walls, white Brahma bulls

slumber among birch trees:
one rises, flops his tongue
across your salty lifeline.

Four brown stallions line up
abreast, galloping behind us
as we peddle into headlights.

A crow peckers pink meat
inside an armadillo's busted shell.
Even Jesus, bleeding

on the splinters,
pleaded to be worshipped
in his sexy swaddling clothes,

age 33, the zenith of his might,
too old to be nervous, too young
not to be naive,

checking us out,
a sun burning
inside closed lids.

Savior Fatso, Semi-Fascist

I bow over a shrub, an evergreen.
I aim my brain down through
the twisted center.

I sure would love to dump
my egomaniac into
this twat

(I horde all my own paintings
of the blood-spackled spread thighs
of mothers suffering abortions)

but I can't feel
the shadows of the needles
pierce that shadow.

Once, my buddy and I dug
holes in the playground
and fucked the dust under the green blades,

laughing about loving our country,
both of us wanting to be lonesome
and invisible, capable

of wandering around the showers,
grabbing every thing, including
that hero who'd just shoved me down stone steps,

who had crooned, "God Bless America" as my hand broke,
who had courted our homecoming queen, that chick
who wore the sweater screaming, "I Am a Machine."

She and I split, somewhat stoned,
to this bend along the Trail of Tears
where snows had forced the tribe

and its saviors
to curl against the cliff
and wait for warmth.

So many froze.
Among the jittering green leaves,
puffs of warm breath.

In this dark bush,
a frail web trembles,
half-intact.

I kneel in mud.
Wildlife scuttles
around the trunk.

Between my knees,
a rat flits free,
my baby leaving me.

A Soft Mad Voice through Black Lipstick

1.

I took my holy father on a date.
A quartet performed Bartok's Fourth.
Around my head, the chapel pulsed
to the pizzicato movement.

"This music's so schizoid,"
I whispered. "I love it."
He flinched, looked down.
"Suck me," he whispered.

Helpless, flaccid, I
curled in his trembling arms;
I eyed the security guard's ass.
Inside my concha, he whispered,

"What on earth should daddy do?"
"Daddy, help me," I whispered.
"I'm swallowing my tongue.
Please stick a pencil in my mouth."

2.

At Shiloh, they found a rifle
stuffed with balls and charges,
the boy too scared to shoot
before being made love to

by two bayonets
on a stained video screen

in a bookstore
for lost adults.

If and when I'm bashed,
I fear I'll drift away,
sucking in those fists
as one feels trained to.

3.

In some cheap motel, I manipulate myself,
staring, moist-eyed, at the full mirror,
at my own sweating sculpture.

4.

In a sauna, a force field lifts.
Across from me, a waving clown
in frantic fuschia pantaloons
seems ready to tweak a copper's nose,

pull me by this stretching hand out
onto banana peels, this cold cement,
both of us skidding in slow motion
toward nude laughers, our religion.

A Virgin Nymphomaniac as Antenna

See this scar across my wrist?
It's from an infantile encounter

with a rose thorn,
not an escape attempt.

I wander hallways, rubbing
at it, weeping on it, milking it.

At Dachau, I took a pebble into my pocket.
I wait for a stained glass window I can bust.

On the foot bridge to where the gas chambers
had stood, I knelt, I bowed.

My head's shadow emerged on the quick flow.
Minnows congregated in my silhouette.

I should have thrust my pulse
into that frigid liquid knife

and let this warm air warm me up,
my flesh antenna blazing

with fresh heat
ghosts could caress,

tourists
in a petting zoo

on some tired day
in yet another everlasting city.

The Red Dust Flesh as Brand New Filter

1. Arroyo Hondo

In my binoculars, a Hell's Angel nods,
tugging down his leather sleeve, rubbing
the black curls upon a classic chest.
Should we go down in the hot spring?

At the cliff's edge, in a pup tent,
a hippie couple fucks, the girl on top,
her bags hanging down over her old man's
buried smile? I salute. She waves.

I elevate my gaze. On that close peak,
a white dogwood petal of spring snow
shrouds a ski slope,
has not shrunk back.

I trip down into a prickly cactus flower's
emerald calyx. A swirling funnel
of small ants sucks sugar, lifting
it out, back home to their hole.

Suddenly, around my toes, this sage falls away.
I nearly faint into the gorge, a horse
dragging a laden cart, its driver
having awakened in time.

The Rio's brown surface seems flat,
its facets catching high-noon light,
igniting into white smoke roils at the falls,
confetti-colored kayaks twirling in those rapids,

little swallows flitting around from cliff
to cliff down there, a family's laughter
echoing up the gorge sides
through perfumed, plush sage.

2. Kilkenny, Whittier, Idyllwild

In the old world, I whistled, wrapped
in a sweat-drenched black sweater
adorned with dry blades, a jackdaw
shrieking my way from a quaking nest;

a passing lass laughed at me as I danced
over a Roman bridge, its crumbling stones
festooned with pink teacup roses, some
having tumbled to the freshet down

below, its crystal muscles curving
over boulders, green weeds waving
in the depths like the tresses
of a drowned girl. Oh, just

ignore me: I grew up near ruins, a fat brat
drowning in the perfume, like herbed dust,
of eucalyptus trees; I loved even
the polluted sunset's salmon glow.

In a torched-down house's foundations, I
played with my dead brother, whispering lies
about two dykes who'd fiddled with each other,
that fateful night, in the bathtub, its lion-

paw feet still clinging to the charred
Formica floor tiles we played war games on,
guarding the vacant lot we felt would be
where the gods' chariots would be.

Naked, we climbed twin gray rocks.
I sprawled back on mine like Prometheus.
He stood, arms extended, radiating
every which way in the bright

dawn, his red locks bursting
with fire, his whole
body a match
I blow

out

3. Charlotte

Little ghost kneeling
in the corner, pray tell me,
is pleasure in here, in this skull, or out

here, where what you hear
in Earth's skull is all
one gets?

Quivering naked against a black mailbox,
a lizard's cold corpse pressed up into my nude sole,
a warm mouse scampering over my other foot's arch,

I witness a station wagon slowly crush
the driver's side door of my parked Pinto
as if breaking my heart, taking my breath away.

At her driveway's end, a stumpy old lawyer lady
pats the summons tucked in her butt pocket.
I should come inside her pup tent.

Because I am human, therefore haunted,
I would sooner throw down the red rose
of my essence, the open

wound of my blooming heart,
upon her toenail,
sexy and red.

4. Sangre de Cristo

Parked alone at a rest stop in a high meadow
I record the murmuring of snowmelt flowing down these slopes
drowning an anthill the fallen
fenceposts having been jiggled

by breeze or hand
after erosion ate the soil
like gums receding
around loose teeth

in my clamped-shut maw laughing loudly in this mind
watching me firing hot gold piss into a hissing snowpatch
I won't get to film muffling me
when my death melts away

5. Moreland

I remember grandpa screaming for more oats,
hunched in his wheeled throne under the Christmas tree,
its red bulbs twinkling
in his smudged lenses

like tracer bullets, half
his low jaw gnawed off

by a crab. Why
did I not ease his body bitterness?

He could have toured my paint and coatings factory
transforming scrap iron into pigment powder.
Birdcages, rusting, smell like sweetened mud,
the brittle scent of ozone in light rain;

on the back dock, scarlet powder had spilled
from a stabbed bag, tinting red the dust
kicked up all over these new white pants,
one's iron zipper, and my own hands.

I could have sunk down into his basement
to lift the new filter, that cardboard rectangle,
that thin frame filled with dust-clogged fibers,
from his quaking lap; facing him,

I could have turned, bent
over, screwed that rough outline of my body
into the central air system's gaping duct
sucking new breath in, his whole house alive.

6. Wilbur

Back in school, my best friend Paul and I plotted
apocalyptic epic odes we failed to commence,
inventing a fake Homeric bard, sort of a Sandburg
such as you've seen featured in those documentaries

called "Why Mankind Creates": envision an ancient
white-bearded Santa type crunching desert gravel,
trekking to his shack, introducing to the camera
his toothless friend whom he insists is a genius:

spontaneous reader, my bubble, my brother,
let's go meet that kind old lover,
our role model, his dreamy body
a weak bridge away from suicide.

The Contemporary Poetry Series

EDITED BY PAUL ZIMMER

Dannie Abse, *One-Legged on Ice*
Susan Astor, *Dame*
Gerald Barrax, *An Audience of One*
Tony Connor, *New and Selected Poems*
Franz Douskey, *Rowing Across the Dark*
Lynn Emanuel, *Hotel Fiesta*
John Engels, *Vivaldi in Early Fall*
John Engels, *Weather-Fear: New and Selected Poems, 1958–1982*
Brendan Galvin, *Atlantic Flyway*
Brendan Galvin, *Winter Oysters*
Michael Heffernan, *The Cry of Oliver Hardy*
Michael Heffernan, *To the Wreakers of Havoc*
Conrad Hilberry, *The Moon Seen as a Slice of Pineapple*
X. J. Kennedy, *Cross Ties*
Caroline Knox, *The House Party*
Gary Margolis, *The Day We Still Stand Here*
Michael Pettit, *American Light*
Bin Ramke, *White Monkeys*
J. W. Rivers, *Proud and on My Feet*
Laurie Sheck, *Amaranth*
Myra Sklarew, *The Science of Goodbyes*
Marcia Southwick, *The Night Won't Save Anyone*
Mary Swander, *Succession*
Bruce Weigl, *The Monkey Wars*
Paul Zarzyski, *The Make-Up of Ice*

The Contemporary Poetry Series

EDITED BY BIN RAMKE

J. T. Barbarese, *New Science*
J. T. Barbarese, *Under the Blue Moon*
Scott Cairns, *Figures for the Ghost*
Scott Cairns, *The Translation of Babel*
Richard Chess, *Tekiah*
Richard Cole, *The Glass Children*
Martha Collins, *A History of a Small Life on a Windy Planet*

Martin Corless-Smith, *Of Piscator*
Christopher Davis, *The Patriot*
Juan Delgado, *Green Web*
Wayne Dodd, *Echoes of the Unspoken*
Wayne Dodd, *Sometimes Music Rises*
Joseph Duemer, *Customs*
Candice Favilla, *Cups*
Casey Finch, *Harming Others*
Norman Finkelstein, *Restless Messengers*
Dennis Finnell, *Belovèd Beast*
Karen Fish, *The Cedar Canoe*
Albert Goldbarth, *Heaven and Earth: A Cosmology*
Pamela Gross, *Birds of the Night Sky/Stars of the Field*
Kathleen Halme, *Every Substance Clothed*
Jonathan Holden, *American Gothic*
Paul Hoover, *Viridian*
Austin Hummell, *The Fugitive Kind*
Claudia Keelan, *The Secularist*
Maurice Kilwein Guevara, *Postmortem*
Caroline Knox, *To Newfoundland*
Steve Kronen, *Empirical Evidence*
Patrick Lawler, *A Drowning Man Is Never Tall Enough*
Sydney Lea, *No Sign*
Jeanne Lebow, *The Outlaw James Copeland and the Champion-Belted Empress*
Phillis Levin, *Temples and Fields*
Gary Margolis, *Falling Awake*
Mark McMorris, *The Black Reeds*
Jacqueline Osherow, *Conversations with Survivors*
Jacqueline Osherow, *Looking for Angels in New York*
Tracy Philpot, *Incorrect Distances*
Donald Revell, *The Gaza of Winter*
Martha Ronk, *Eyetrouble*
Martha Clare Ronk, *Desire in L.A.*
Aleda Shirley, *Chinese Architecture*
Pamela Stewart, *The Red Window*
Susan Stewart, *The Hive*
Terese Svoboda, *All Aberration*
Terese Svoboda, *Mere Mortals*
Lee Upton, *Approximate Darling*
Arthur Vogelsang, *Twentieth Century Women*
Sidney Wade, *Empty Sleeves*
Marjorie Welish, *Casting Sequences*
Susan Wheeler, *Bag 'o' Diamonds*
C. D. Wright, *String Light*